The
**Faith in
Action**
Series

Changing the Face of Death

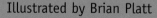

The Story of Cicely Saunders

Shirley du Boulay

A new edition with additional material
by Louisa Wagg and Catherine Bowness

Illustrated by Brian Platt

RMEP

RELIGIOUS AND MORAL EDUCATION PRESS

CHANGING THE FACE OF DEATH

The Story of Cicely Saunders

Cicely Saunders met David Tasma in 1947, when she was twenty-nine. For years she had lived with a feeling of expectation, of something good around the corner. She longed to love someone and be loved in return. At last it had happened, but David had cancer, an incurable kind of cancer, and he was dying.

David had come to England as a Jewish refugee from Warsaw and he had no family or friends. He was only forty and he was dying in great pain. Until he met Cicely, David had been extremely lonely. He felt that his life had been wasted because it had made no difference to the world.

Cicely was a hospital social worker. She visited David as often as she could and when he felt strong enough they talked quietly. David asked Cicely to say 'something to comfort me' and, because he was Jewish, Cicely quoted as much as she could remember from the Psalms. When she could remember no more, she suggested reading other Psalms from a book containing the Psalms and the New Testament that she carried with her. She has never forgotten David's reply, 'I only want what is in your mind and in your heart.'

In most hospitals at that time, incurable patients received very little special care. Doctors believed that their job was to cure disease. A patient who could not be cured represented a failure to them. Very little research was done into the care of the dying. Many patients were terrified of dying and worried about what would happen to their families. Some were kept heavily drugged to deaden the pain, which meant that they remained half-asleep until they died.

Cicely and David thought that even if such people could not be cured, surely they could be cared for more lovingly, more efficiently. They should be allowed to die peacefully, without pain or fear.

Cicely wondered whether *she* could do something about it. Perhaps she could research into improved methods of controlling pain? Gradually an idea took shape. She would build a special hospital for people at the end of their lives, a welcoming place with highly trained staff to give the patients all the skilful treatment and loving care they needed.

David was thrilled by Cicely's idea. If something like that could come about because of him, maybe there would have been some point to his life after all. He decided to help Cicely in a practical way. He made his will and left her £500, almost all that he had. 'I'll be a window in your home,' he told her.

Soon afterwards, David died. Shattered by his death, Cicely made up her mind to build a home around the window David had left her. 'If God calls, he also enables,' she believed. God had inspired her with the idea of building a home for the dying, so he would make her dream possible, but it took nineteen years.

From the start she accepted three challenges. First she realized that David's 'window' was also an opening leading her towards the greater task of changing the face of death for more people than she could help in her home alone. Secondly, she realized that to care properly for the dying the doctor's scientific knowledge must be combined with caring love. The mind and the heart must work together. Thirdly, through her love for somebody of a different faith from her own, Cicely understood that there are many ways for people to find their own truth. She and her helpers should respect that every person makes their own journey, in their own way.

What Do You Think?

Important: In answering 'What Do You Think?' questions in this book, it is important that you not only state your opinion but also give as many reasons as possible for your opinion.

1. Cicely longed to fall in love and be loved in return. David had been lonely until he met Cicely. Do all human beings need to be loved? Is there a difference between liking someone and loving them?

2. David felt that his whole life had been wasted. Why do you think he felt this and was there any justification for this feeling? Is any human life ever wasted?

3. We are often told that the health service has very little money to spare. Should money be spent to ease the suffering of people who are dying or would it be better spent on researching diseases and conditions which cause death in order to find a cure?

4. How did David's window become an opening for Cicely? What were the challenges she accepted? David's short life is remembered by this window and by the work which it inspired. How would you like to be remembered?

Training to be a Nurse

Cicely Saunders was born on 22 June 1918 in Barnet, a few miles north of London. She had two younger brothers, John and Christopher. The family was well off and there were all sorts of things Cicely could do at home, like riding and playing tennis and squash. But her parents' marriage was an unhappy one. Although they never quarrelled in public, the atmosphere was always strained. Naturally, this affected the children. Cicely was unhappy at boarding-school too. The fact that she was much taller than the other girls made her shy and awkward and she had very few friends.

When she left school she found it difficult to choose a career. Earlier on she had wanted to be a nurse, but her parents had discouraged her. Now she decided to go to Oxford University and study politics, philosophy and economics, thinking that this would be useful if she became secretary to a politician, a job she thought she might enjoy.

For a while her studies went well, but when the Second World War broke out in 1939 she knew it was time to do something more practical and useful. Disregarding her parents' advice, she left Oxford and enrolled for nursing training at St Thomas's Hospital, London.

Here Cicely fitted in at once and became one of the most popular and successful of the student nurses. Realizing that she had the makings of an excellent nurse, the staff expected a great deal from her and pushed her hard. Cicely still remembers one sister who used to chase her up and down the wards. 'You *can* be good and you *will* be good. That is why I chase you!' she told Cicely.

Nursing is tiring and difficult work, and it was particularly exhausting for Cicely because she suffered from backache. Her spine was slightly crooked, and while she was at boarding-school she had been made to lie flat on the floor for forty minutes a day.

So when her training ended, Cicely went to see a surgeon about her back. He told her she must stop nursing altogether. Bitterly disappointed, Cicely made up her mind to stay as close to patients as she could by becoming a hospital social worker, or almoner as it was then called. This was a very practical job. It involved arranging convalescent homes for patients coming out of hospital, making sure that patients' families were managing all right and were not short of money, and also helping them find their own strengths to control what was happening.

Becoming a Christian

While she was training to be a hospital social worker, Cicely became a Christian. For a long time, she had been searching for faith without success. Then, one day while she was on holiday in Cornwall, she discovered that she really believed. It was, she said, 'as if a switch had flipped'. She was deeply happy and wanted to do something to thank God immediately but it wasn't until she met David Tasma, three years later, that Cicely understood that her way of thanking and serving God would be to work with dying people.

After David's death Cicely continued her hospital social work and also became a volunteer sister at St Luke's Hospital, a home for the dying in Bayswater, London. However, it wasn't enough for Cicely to be with the dying in the evenings. She asked the doctor she was working for whether she could be a night nurse. Perhaps that wouldn't strain her back too much? He replied that if she really wanted to help, she must become a doctor. 'Go and read medicine,' he said. 'They won't listen to you as a nurse. It's the doctors who desert the dying. There's so much more to be learnt about pain and you'll only be frustrated if you don't do it properly.'

Cicely took his advice. She was already thirty-three and much older than the other medical students. She felt very out of place, especially when she overheard one of them say, 'She'll be ninety before she qualifies!' Cicely wasn't easily put off, however, and qualified as a doctor before she was forty.

In 1958, soon after qualifying, Cicely obtained a research scholarship at St Mary's Hospital, Paddington. This gave her the opportunity to study the treatment of pain in the incurably ill. Then she arranged to go to St Joseph's, a hospice for the dying run by nuns, for three days a week. Besides listening to the patients, helping the nuns to care for them more skilfully, and learning as much as she could, Cicely developed record-keeping methods and took scientific research notes on eleven hundred patients, using what was then a modern punch-card system.

What Do You Think?

1. Cicely became a Christian when she was on holiday in Cornwall. Why do people often make big decisions when they are away from home and work?

2. When a person feels called by God to do something, they often say it's a vocation. What types of activity might be classed as vocational?

3. What did the doctor mean when he said that it was doctors who deserted the dying? Was this a fair statement? Try to give an example to support your point of view.

4. When Cicely went to St Joseph's, why was it vital for her research for her to listen to patients and to keep good records about them?

Pain Control

At St Joseph's Cicely introduced the skilful system of giving drugs for pain relief that she had discovered at St Luke's. There, instead of waiting until a patient was in agony and crying out for help, staff gave painkillers regularly, usually every four hours. In this way the patients received their drugs before the pain returned, and didn't become tense and anxious waiting for the effects of the last dose to wear off. This was so effective that it became the normal practice at St Joseph's.

One patient admitted to St Joseph's from another hospital told Cicely about the enormous difference that regular injections had made:

> They used to try to see how long I could go without an injection. I used to be pouring with sweat because of the pain. I couldn't speak to anyone and I was having crying fits. I think I've only cried once since I've been here, that's well over a week. ... The biggest difference is feeling so calm. I don't get worked up. I don't get upset, I don't get very depressed. Really black thoughts were going through my mind. Since I've been here I've been more hopeful.

Cicely's studies also made her aware that besides their pain-killing effects, drugs can successfully treat common complaints of the dying, such as bedsores, nausea, depression, constipation and breathlessness.

All this experience would prove invaluable in later years. Meanwhile, Cicely's plans for the hospice she dreamed of building grew clearer and more detailed.

What Do You Think?

1. What treatment gave patients more hope at St Joseph's Hospice? Why did they not feel so hopeful in ordinary hospital wards? Why might this treatment not be appropriate for all patients in hospital?

2. Why was Cicely's experience at St Joseph's so invaluable to her and how did it prepare her for the future?

The Dream Becomes Reality

The word 'hospice', like 'hospital', comes from the Latin word *hospes*, which means both 'host' and 'guest'. There were hospices as long ago as the fourth century C.E. In the Middle Ages monasteries ran hospices where travellers could stop and rest before continuing their journey. The monks also looked after the sick, wounded or dying. It was not until the late nineteenth century that a hospice came to mean a place primarily for the dying, and there were very few real hospices even then. So when Cicely planned her hospice she was reviving something very old, but in a completely new way.

How does one woman, however well-qualified and energetic, set out to build a hospice? Cicely had calculated that she would need about half a million pounds, and all she had was David Tasma's £500!

In 1959 Cicely wrote thousands of letters to everyone she could think of who might be interested in helping with the project and began fund-raising in earnest. Carefully and tactfully, she wrote to charitable trusts, large companies and other organizations, and asked for donations and loans, often asking for a specific sum.

In her letters Cicely would outline her plans for the hospice. She started by describing how well dying patients were treated at St Joseph's, then went on to say that she intended to do something similar but to include research and education so that knowledge and care could be spread. She already knew how many beds she wanted in the hospice, what kind of staff would work there and, above all, the atmosphere they would try to achieve: warm and caring, like a friendly village.

Cicely and her helpers decided to name the hospice after St Christopher, the patron saint of travellers. They hoped this would act as a reminder that death is part of the journey through life. Nearly half of the patients who come to St Christopher's Hospice are able to go home again, sometimes for quite a long time, but some come there to die.

St Christopher's Hospice was registered as a charity and money began to arrive, sometimes large cheques from charitable trusts, sometimes just a pound or two from someone who wanted to help.

In 1963, before she had collected any more money, Cicely decided it was time to take the plunge and start building. She went to look at a site in Sydenham, South London that she had heard was for sale.

It was a building plot where two houses had been knocked down. The location was ideal: there were bus-stops and railway stations nearby, but the area was not too built-up or noisy. The patients would be able to sit and watch people and traffic going by, and their families and friends would be able to visit them easily. There was plenty of room for the garden Cicely had in mind, and even some beautiful mature trees. Cicely didn't want to build her hospice in the depths of the country, where the patients might feel isolated; she felt it was important for them not to be shut off from ordinary life.

After a struggle, enough money was raised to buy the site and the builders started work. It was a very exciting time, but very worrying too. At one stage the money ran out. They needed an extra £100 000. 'That's £1000 for every day except Sundays from now until Christmas,' Cicely said to a friend.

The early 1960s were extremely busy years for her. In addition to supervising the building and dealing with all the problems of fund-raising, Cicely was still working at St Joseph's. In 1963 she went on a 'voyage of discovery' to the United States, where they were ahead in pain research, and came home elated and encouraged. Then in 1965 she left St Joseph's to write and lecture about the care of the dying, travelling all over Britain and abroad.

At last, after some nerve-racking set-backs, the hospice was finished, with a window dedicated to David Tasma.

The building was ready. Now it had to be fitted out. The hospice filled up with heaps of bedding, crockery, curtains, beds, chairs, kitchen and medical equipment, bedpans and even a fish-tank as Cicely thought patients would find it relaxing to watch the fish. Nurses rushed about, moving furniture and making beds. Gangs of children weeded the flower-beds. The fire brigade, for some reason now forgotten, hung the curtains! For a while it was chaos, but in the end everything was in place for the opening on 24 July 1967. This was performed by Princess Alexandra, who later became patron of St Christopher's and who, at her own request, continues to visit the hospice just before Christmas each year.

Cicely in 1996 sitting beside the window dedicated to David Tasma.

What Do You Think?

1. The idea of a hospice is a very old one. What other ideas from past times have been revived? What ideas from our own time may interest future generations?

2. Cicely raised funds to add to David's £500. What do you think is the most successful way of raising money?

3. Cicely took care to outline her plans for the hospice to possible sponsors. Why is it important to share plans with those who may provide funding for special projects?

4. The new hospice was named after St Christopher to remind people of the idea of travelling. Many religious people speak of life and death as being part of a journey. What do you think they mean and is this a good image to choose? How would you describe life?

5. What reasons might Cicely give for not shutting the dying away from ordinary life? The first hospice was to have an atmosphere like a 'friendly village'. What features does a village have which are similar to those Cicely wanted for her hospice?

6. When the hospice was finished, a window was dedicated in memory of David. Why do you think it was important to Cicely to keep her promise to her dying friend? How do you think she felt at the dedication ceremony? Have you ever tried to keep an important promise made to a friend? If so, what made you make the effort to keep that promise?

St Christopher's Hospice

The wards in the hospice are roomy and pleasant, each divided into rooms of four beds, with plenty of single rooms for patients who need privacy, such as those with young families. Everything is cheerful and comfortable with pretty curtains and carpets, and interesting paintings on the walls. There is also a day centre where patients come from home, or from the wards. Here they can reminisce or do more creative things such as painting, pottery and writing. Often they make presents for their families.

Cicely planned St Christopher's very carefully, making sure that even those patients who had to stay in bed could move around without difficulty. There are lifts as well as stairs and all the doorways and corridors are wide enough for beds as well as wheelchairs to go through. Even the bathrooms are large enough for patients' beds to be wheeled in.

The chapel is right at the centre of the building. It is a peaceful, plain room, with plenty of chairs and room for beds and wheelchairs.

Cicely envisaged St Christopher's as a living community, a place where people of all ages live together, not simply a place where people go when they are ill. The first people to move into the hospice temporarily took up residence in the wing for the elderly, and for the next thirty years the Drapers' Wing, as it became known, provided accommodation for elderly former staff, relatives of staff and volunteers who were having difficulty in coping by themselves. However, because the work of St Christopher's has expanded into home care and other fields, the Drapers' Wing has now been closed and the original playgroup for the children of the staff has become an official nursery.

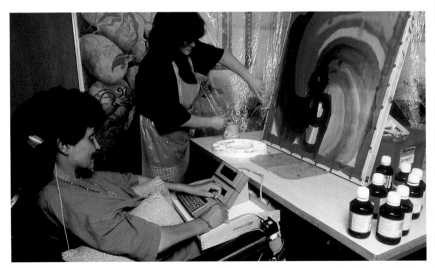

A patient at St Christopher's enjoys silk-screen painting with the help of a volunteer.

What Do You Think?

1. Cicely planned the hospice with her patients in mind. If you were designing a room in a hospice, what would be the three most important features you would put on your plan?

2. Why do you think Cicely placed a chapel at the centre of the building?

3. Cicely wanted the hospice to be a living community not just a place where people go when they are ill. How do you think this attitude might help (a) those who are patients, (b) their family and friends?

More Like a Home than a Hospital

When a patient arrives at St Christopher's, someone from the team who will care for him, or her, comes down to the entrance to greet the patient by name and take them and their relatives up to the ward. The other patients, the nurses and any visitors or volunteer helpers are introduced. It is a good way to be welcomed.

St Christopher's is very flexible; patients don't have to arrive at a set time, and sometimes arrangements are altered even at the last minute. When one very ill young woman arrived, the doctor she spoke to realized she was unhappy about something. It turned out that the patient was upset at having to miss her best friend's birthday party, which was on the day she was due to be admitted to St Christopher's. The staff encouraged her to go and enjoy the party and come on to the hospice afterwards. Very cheered by this, she did as they suggested and arrived at the hospice after the party finally ended – at three o'clock in the morning!

Another of the things that has always made St Christopher's more like a home than a hospital is that people can visit the patients more or less when they like. There are no fixed visiting-hours. Visitors can drop in just as they would drop in on a friend at home. Of course they try not to choose an inconvenient time, when the patients are asleep or having lunch, for example.

It is quite common to see a patient's bed completely surrounded by friends and relatives, the children playing on the floor and everyone chatting and drinking tea and eating cakes (probably provided by St Christopher's kitchen staff). There are lots of parties at the hospice too, especially when there is a birthday or wedding anniversary to celebrate.

Even animals may come and visit! A circus owner once brought a baby elephant with him when he came to see his father. No one objected but as the elephant couldn't fit into the lift, the sick man came down to reception to see him!

A patient, a nurse and a hospice volunteer join forces.

What Do You Think?

1. How does St Christopher's flexible timetable help new patients?

2. Why is it important for a hospice to be like a home?

3. Why do you think visitors are allowed to bring animals into the hospice?

The Nurses

Cicely has always paid great attention to small details because she knows how much they matter when you are ill. She never wore a stethoscope when she visited the wards as she felt that patients would rather look at an attractive string of beads or a brooch than a medical instrument. The flowers are always fresh and nicely arranged, the kitchen staff try to serve everyone food they like and the patients can have their hair washed and their fingers manicured when they want to.

Friendly care is still very important despite the fact that nowadays both nursing staff and doctors have specialist training in the care of the dying and that there is now much more that can be done to treat the symptoms of illness.

Having been a nurse, Cicely knows what nursing involves. The doctors decide how each person is to be treated, but it is the nurses who carry out the treatment. Cicely encourages them to think for themselves and to work closely with the doctors. Their suggestions are always welcomed.

While the nurses work hard for the physical comfort of the patients, bathing eyes gently, washing out sore mouths and rubbing soothing cream on rough elbows, they also pay great attention to personal details. They will spend a long time rearranging a patient's pillows until he or she is perfectly comfortable, for instance, or adjusting the position of the television set

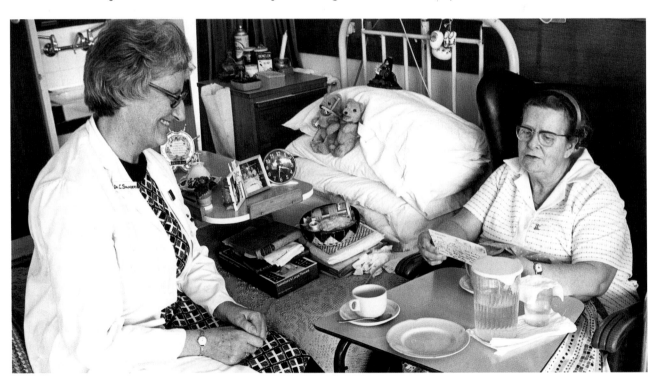

A patient shares a postcard with Cicely.

for someone who can't move his head easily. The patient's notes act as a reminder of their needs and wishes: one would like her clock wound twice a day, another wants the curtains drawn in the afternoon, to protect his eyes from the bright sunlight, and another prefers to sleep with her crucifix in her hand.

Most important of all, the nurses give their time. However busy they are, they are never too busy to stop and talk. People who are ill have all sorts of fears; they need a relaxed, friendly atmosphere to be able to discuss their worries and even their aims, for it is surprising how much can be fitted into a few remaining weeks or days. Inessentials fall away and nothing matters more than family and friends.

On one occasion, a male social worker came across a teenage girl swearing horribly in the corridor. 'They're all being so *nice* to my father, and he's been so *horrid* to me,' she explained. The social worker advised her to go and tell her father how she felt. She followed his advice and found she was able to share her feelings with her father. Tragic circumstances can sometimes help communication, even between teenagers and parents who have not found it easy to talk to each other before.

What Do You Think?

1. Why did Cicely refuse to wear a stethoscope on her visits to the wards?

2. Cicely felt that it was very important to listen to the wishes of her dying patients. Today people who have a terminal illness are often encouraged to do whatever they wish, e.g. eat their favourite foods, or spend their savings on a special holiday. Why are they given this advice? How may this help them and their families cope with knowing that they cannot be cured?

3. Why is it important for the hospice workers to give their time to patients?

4. What sorts of fears might dying people have? What questions might they want to ask the hospice staff?

5. Why do you think the girl who was swearing was upset? Why do teenagers and their parents sometimes find it difficult to talk to each other?

Total Pain

As Cicely learned at St Joseph's, pain is not only physical. There are several ways of feeling pain. One day a patient at St Joseph's had told her: 'It began in my back, but now it seems that all of me is wrong. I began to cry for the pills and injections but I knew that I mustn't. The whole world seemed to be against me. Nobody seemed to understand. My husband and son were marvellous, but they were having to stay off work and lose their money. It's marvellous to begin to feel safe again.'

Before she came to the hospice, this woman was not only in physical pain, she was feeling helpless and isolated; Cicely calls this 'emotional pain'. She was worried about her family and whether they had enough money, too; Cicely calls this 'social pain'. Her longing to feel safe and find some sort of meaning to life Cicely calls 'spiritual pain'.

Cicely's name for this state, made up of at least three kinds of pain, is 'total pain'. She realizes that it isn't enough to treat the physical pain alone, although this is important. The whole person is suffering, so the whole person must be treated. St Christopher's does just that.

What Do You Think?

1. Explain in a few phrases what Cicely meant by 'total pain'.

2. 'Treating the whole person' is a phrase which is becoming common today. What do you think it means?

Religion

The hospice staff need not practise any religion, although some of them do. Everyone is welcome and treated with warmth and affection whatever they believe or don't believe. A nurse who worked at St Christopher's for a while wrote: 'I expected to see patients being cared for. The surprise was to find myself automatically included in people's perceptive loving and caring.'

All the staff are prepared to talk about important subjects. 'We don't talk about "religion" here, but we are always meeting people who want to talk deeply,' explains Cicely. The staff know that people near death often worry about life after death, and wonder whether God

A ward clerk has time to listen and laugh with a patient.

exists and if there is any meaning to life. 'Well, I don't understand either,' a nurse may say to a patient, 'but I'm trying to. Let's talk about it and see if we can help each other a little.' St Christopher's staff may not have all the answers, but they are always ready to listen, or to be still and give the patients space to do their own thinking. 'The way care is given can reach the most hidden places' is a favourite quote of Cicely's.

There are religious services in the chapel on Sundays and, during the week, patients may call for Communion or blessings on the ward. Many patients or their families who haven't been to church for years find comfort in simple, long-remembered words, particularly at the monthly Service of Thanks.

What Do You Think?

1. What do you think Cicely means when she says, 'We don't talk about religion here but we are always meeting people who want to talk deeply'? Why do the hospice workers have to be prepared to talk about important subjects?

2. Why do people often begin to think about religious questions when they know their life is almost over?

Personal Involvement

Cicely was deeply impressed by David Tasma's remark, 'I want what is in your mind and in your heart' (page 2). As she understood it, David meant that he needed not only her knowledge of modern medicine and the treatment of pain, but her personal involvement as well. He wanted those around him to care about him as a person, to be friendly as well as efficient. For this reason Cicely tries to employ people who are cheerful, hard-working and friendly. They must also be willing to listen and learn.

People who work with the sick and dying and their families can find it rewarding and interesting to get to know them well, but there are drawbacks to this kind of commitment. They risk feeling the loss more bitterly if the patient dies, and they face painful questions like 'My husband's so young. How shall I bear it when he dies?'

The hardest question of all to answer is 'Am I dying?' In the past, doctors tended to make it a rule never to admit to a dying patient that they would not recover, even if asked point-blank. It seemed to Cicely and others that this was unfair and even cruel. When a member of the hospice staff is asked 'Am I dying?' or 'Am I going to get better?' they try to find out whether the patient is ready for the truth. They let the patient guide the conversation, often by answering with another question. For example, 'What makes you think you might be dying?' or 'Why do you ask me that? You've only just arrived here.' In many cases the dying patient has already guessed the truth. Knowing for certain can help them prepare for death calmly, without fear or confusion.

What Do You Think?

1. David Tasma told Cicely that he wanted 'what is in your mind and in your heart'. Why did these words make such an impression on Cicely and what did she think they meant?

2. If you worked in a hospice, what task do you think you would find most difficult?

Bereavement

Cicely understands what it is like to be bereaved. Over the years she has lost many close friends. She knows that the pain of losing someone you love can last a very long time.

St Christopher's looks after the families of people who are dying as well as the patients themselves. There are social workers there to give practical assistance, such as advising on grants available to families who are short of money, making sure they have a telephone (this can be essential when someone is seriously ill), organizing meals on wheels and other community help, and even arranging holidays for patients and their families.

One of the most valuable contributions these social workers make is to comfort and support bereaved people, simply by listening and talking to them. If necessary, they can arrange a meeting with a 'bereavement counsellor', a person specially trained to help those who have lost a member of the family or a friend. Also a meeting is held each month at St Christopher's for the recently bereaved. Here people who are suffering find that sharing their problems and experiences in a group can be a great help. Professional advice is available at these sessions, which are also attended by the Chaplain.

St Christopher's has a special concern for children who lose parents or grandparents. They distribute information leaflets, hold meetings and provide help for children, teachers and other family members when young people in the area have been bereaved.

The chapel at St Christopher's is regularly crowded with scores of people who have returned on the first anniversary of a patient's death. In a simple Service of Thanks candles are lit, names read out and notes are brought by the families. Children are particularly welcome. After listening to a story they blow out the candles, which they can take home to light on special occasions. More than half the people who come to these services are not in touch with the Church, but even so they find that hymns and prayers can help their own thoughts.

What Do You Think?

1. Who needs the most help from a hospice, the dying patients or their relatives?

2. Why do you think people find comfort in the lighting of a candle? What might these candles symbolize?

Home Care

Cheerful, comfortable and homely though the hospice is, some people prefer to stay at home for as long as possible. They may even want to die at home. Looking after someone who is very ill can be frightening for their relatives, so in 1969 Cicely and her staff started a Home Care Team who, working closely with local doctors, visit patients at home. This gives the patients the best of both worlds: the special skills of St Christopher's in the familiar surroundings of their own homes.

Home Care has grown enormously since 1969, both at St Christopher's and nationally through Macmillan Nurses and the Marie Curie Foundation. The ratio of patients being looked after at St Christopher's and at home has changed dramatically. Now there are just forty patients being cared for in St Christopher's itself, while about five hundred are being cared for in their own homes. Not only do these patients enjoy the skills of the Home Care Team, but they are full members of the St Christopher's family. Many of them attend the day centre and if they want to, or need to, they may have a bed at the hospice.

Ethel, an elderly and chronically ill woman, had asked her husband to promise not to put her in a hospital. However, it was often difficult for him to look after her by himself. Whenever he was worried about a problem, he would ring up one of the Home Care sisters. They either gave him advice over the telephone or came round to help. Towards the end of Ethel's life the nurses were visiting her twice a day. She grew very fond of them. Ethel died a few minutes after one of the nurses arrived one day. 'She waited for you to come,' said her husband.

A Home Care nurse visiting a patient at home.

What Do You Think?

1. Why might some terminally ill people prefer to spend their last days at home?

2. What difficulties might a carer face when looking after a dying relative at home? What support might such a carer need?

The Hospice Movement

When she built St Christopher's Hospice, Cicely did not realize that she had already started a new movement. She had seen that dying people were not given enough care and attention and she had done something about it. But soon others began to follow her example. They built more hospices and set up home-care teams of their own, or simply put her ideas into practice in the hospitals where they worked. Now Cicely is recognized as the founder of the modern hospice movement. She has received many honours and awards. In 1980 she became a Dame, and in 1989 the Queen gave her the Order of Merit, which is the only decoration that is a personal gift of the monarch.

St Christopher's was the first hospice to work successfully in four different areas: it looks after patients in wards at the hospice; it operates a home-care service; it does a great deal of teaching and it carries out research into the treatment of the dying. At St Christopher's hundreds of thousands of pieces of information are collected: from letters, hospital records and doctors' and nurses' notes. The information is stored and then made available for analysis and research.

There are now hospices in about ninety countries throughout the world, but St Christopher's remains a pioneer, always looking at new ways of helping its patients and their families.

Cicely is delighted by the spread of the hospice movement and the way that it is now looking beyond the relief of cancer, motor neuron disease and AIDS to other diseases. What she would like now, above all, is to see her way of treating the dying become part of ordinary health care everywhere. She wants all hospital patients to receive the same care as hospice patients.

What Do You Think?

1. There are now hospices all over the world. Why do you think Cicely is trying to encourage hospitals to use similar care methods?

Cicely receiving an award at a university in Canada in 1997.

Cicely Now

In 1980 Cicely married Marian Bohusz, a Polish professor of art. She says she fell in love with his paintings before she even met him. In 1963 she bought one of Marian's pictures, showing 'Christ stilling the storm', at an exhibition of his work. She wrote to thank him for painting such a beautiful picture and explained that she was going to put it in her hospice. This pleased Marian very much. Soon afterwards they met and fell in love.

However, Marian was already married. His wife lived in Poland and he had not seen her since the Second World War, when he had been captured and imprisoned by the Germans. It was not until his wife had died, when he was seventy-nine and Cicely was sixty-one, that Marian felt at liberty to remarry. They loved each other very deeply and were very happy together for fifteen years until Marian's death in 1995.

Cicely still leads a very full life. Although she is in her eighties she goes to St Christopher's every day, when possible, she writes about the care of the dying and travels the world to tell people about the hospice movement. She has achieved a great deal since David Tasma died. She has made it possible for hundreds of people to die peacefully, without pain, fear or unhappiness. One woman who arrived at St Christopher's when she was near death was asked how she felt. She replied, 'I've never been so happy in my life.'

Cicely's work has led to a real change in the way people think about the dying throughout the field of medicine and nursing, but she is very modest about her success. She simply believes she was the right person in the right place at the right time. She did what she thought God wanted her to do.

Cicely with her husband Marian.

Biographical Notes

Cicely Saunders was born in Barnet, London, on 22 June 1918. After boarding-school she studied philosophy, politics and economics at Oxford. After a year she left to become a nurse. Her nursing training began in 1940. She qualified in 1944 but had to give up nursing because of back trouble. She returned to Oxford to study political theory and public and social administration as part of her training to be an almoner, which was completed in 1947. She had become a Christian in 1945. During her training she started working as a volunteer at St Luke's Hospital, Bayswater, a home for the dying. This work continued until 1958.

At the age of thirty-three Cicely began training to be a doctor at St Thomas's Hospital Medical School, London, qualifying in 1957. Between 1958 and 1965 she carried out research into the care of the terminally ill at St Joseph's Hospice, Hackney. In 1961 St Christopher's Hospice was registered as a charity and in 1967 it was officially opened.

Cicely Saunders and Marian Bohusz were married in 1980.

Her numerous awards include the following:

1969   Honorary Doctor of Science at Yale University

1974   Fellow of the Royal College of Physicians

1977   Lambeth Doctorate of Medicine

1980   Dame of the British Empire

1981   Templeton Prize for Progress in Religion

1987   British Medical Association Gold Medal

1989   Order of Merit

Things to Do

1 Imagine that you are filming a television documentary about the life and work of Cicely Saunders. In the opening scene, Cicely is visiting David in hospital. In the final scene, David's window is unveiled. Briefly outline both scenes and select suitable pieces of background music to enhance the scenes.

2 Some people believe that euthanasia should be made legal in this country. Find out:

(a) what euthanasia means;
(b) which countries allow it;
(c) three arguments in favour of euthanasia and three against it.

3 Imagine you are Cicely. Write a letter to the Director of your local health trust explaining why you believe that the dying need better treatment.

4 Improvise a dramatic sketch based on **one** of the following parts of the story:

(a) Cicely telling her parents that she wishes to become a nurse (page 4)
(b) Cicely visiting the back surgeon after passing her nursing training (page 5)
(c) Cicely meeting the doctor at St Luke's (pages 5–6)

5 Design a prospectus explaining the policies and facilities of an imaginary hospice.

6 Design a window which you would dedicate to someone you love or someone you have loved.

7 Create an advertising campaign for a media appeal to raise funds for building a new hospice.

8 Imagine that you are the parent of a very sick child. A friend has suggested that you contact the local hospice for support. Write a letter to your friend telling them about your first visit to the hospice.

9 Find out where your nearest hospice is and invite a member of staff or fund-raiser to talk to you about their work.

10 Cicely used to read from the Psalms to David to comfort him. Look at the scriptures of any religious tradition and select some words which might comfort (a) the dying, (b) the bereaved **or** choose a piece of modern music which might help a sick person cope with illness.

11 Use local and national newspapers to follow debates about the treatment of the dying. Build up a collection of cuttings and make a scrap-book or search the Internet for recent arguments about care of the terminally ill.

12 Find out what members of at least three religious traditions believe about death and the possibility of life after death. Make a group presentation of your findings.

13 Ask local hospital chaplains or social workers how they try to support the dying and their close relatives.

14 If someone who was ill and in pain asked, 'Why has this happened to me?' what would you say to them and why would you say this?

Questions for Assessment or Examination Candidates

15 'It is better to die with dignity than to go on living in pain.'

With reference to the teachings of at least one religious tradition, explain why people may agree or disagree with this statement.

16 Answer **one** of the following structured questions:

(a) Outline the main aims of the hospice movement. (5 marks)

(b) What did Cicely Saunders mean when she spoke about 'total pain' and how did she help patients through it? (5 marks)

(c) A Christian man and his wife have been married for twenty-five years. They both know that the wife has a painful terminal illness and she asks her husband to help her end her life. Do you think that he should follow his wife's wishes and what religious teachings might he think of as he considers her request? (10 marks)

OR

(a) With reference to any religion you have studied, produce an argument to show that the dying deserve better health care. (10 marks)

(b) What is meant by (i) resurrection, (ii) reincarnation. (5 marks)

(c) Explain why many religious people would support the aims of the hospice movement. (5 marks)

Religious and Moral Education Press
*A division of SCM–Canterbury Press Ltd,
a wholly owned subsidiary of
Hymns Ancient & Modern Ltd
St Mary's Works, St Mary's Plain
Norwich, Norfolk NR3 3BH*

First published 1985

New edition first published 2001

ISBN 1 85175 217 X

Designed and typeset by
TOPICS – The Creative Partnership,
Exeter

Printed in Great Britain by
Brightsea Press, Exeter for
SCM–Canterbury Press Ltd, Norwich

Notes for Teachers

The first Faith in Action books were published in the late 1970s and the series has remained popular with both teachers and pupils. However, much in education has changed over the last twenty years, such as the development of both new examination syllabuses in Religious Studies and local agreed syllabuses for Religious Education which place more emphasis on pupils' own understanding, interpretation and evaluation of religious belief and practice, rather than a simple knowledge of events. This has encouraged us to amend the style of the Faith in Action Series to make it more suitable for today's classroom.

The aim is, as before, to tell the stories of people who have lived and acted according to their faith, but we have included alongside the main story questions which will encourage pupils to think about the reasons for the behaviour of our main characters and to empathize with the situations in which they found themselves. We hope that pupils will also be able to relate some of the issues in the stories to other issues in modern society, either in their own area or on a global scale.

The 'What Do You Think?' questions may be used for group or class discussion or for short written exercises. The 'Things to Do' at the end of the story include ideas for longer activities and more-structured questions suitable for assessment or examination practice.

In line with current syllabus requirements, as Britain is a multifaith society, Faith in Action characters will be selected from a wide variety of faith backgrounds and many of the questions may be answered from the perspective of more than one faith.

CMB, 1997

Acknowledgements

Photographs are reproduced by kind permisson of St Christopher's Hospice and Dame Cicely Saunders, O.M., D.B.E., F.R.C.P.